THIS BOOK BELONGS TO

_____

TABLE OF CONTENTS

GIRLS ARE AMAZING

A COLLECTION OF SHORT STORIES FOR GIRLS ABOUT COURAGE, STRENGTH AND LOVE – PRESENT FOR GIRLS

ANNABELLE LINDGREEN

ISBN – 9798720571818

THE FAIRY DANCE

Ella sat staring at the 10th birthday party invitation in her hand. It had been very nice of her new classmate to invite her to a party, but she didn't feel happy about it at all. The thought of being at a party surrounded by people she didn't know made her feel anxious. She'd tried to hide the invitation before her mother saw it, but she hadn't been quick enough.

"Oh, a party, how lovely!" her mother had said.

"But, Mummy, I don't want to go," Ella had said quietly. "I won't know anyone."

"Nonsense. It'll be a perfect chance to make some new friends," her mother had replied.

Ella had tried to explain that she was scared of going to the party all alone, not to mention the dancing. She hated dancing. It wasn't that she didn't like the music or anything. Really, it was because she had no idea how to dance and she was always worried she'd look silly if she tried. Her mother, however, had simply said she didn't have to dance if she didn't want to. Ella sighed to herself and wondered if she could pretend to be sick on the day of the party. No. She shook her head. She couldn't lie to her mother. There was still a week until the party. Maybe she could try talking to her mother again before then.

The next day was Saturday, so there was no school. Ella decided to go for a walk in the woods close to her home and think of a way to avoid the party. She told her mother where she was going, packed a little bag of snacks and a drink, and set off. While Ella was shy around people, she felt completely at home in the woods and soon relaxed as she walked amongst the trees.

Despite being spring, Ella was warm enough in her light jacket. She skipped along the woodland track, enjoying the sunlight streaming through the trees and throwing dappled shade all around. The scent of last night's rain filled the air, and she took a deep breath. Everything felt so fresh. Thoughts of the party began to melt away as she explored the trail.

As Ella began to climb a slight hill, she suddenly heard the sound of music drifting through the air. She wondered who could be playing music in the middle of the woods. Curious, she crept closer, following the sound. Just over the rise, she saw a strange clearing. The open area was surrounded by old oak trees and tall standing stones covered with patches of moss and strange circular carvings.

Ella crouched down, realising there were people in the clearing. They seemed to be preparing for some sort of party. Several musicians were tuning their instruments, and others were placing food on long benches draped with fine, pale cloth. Ella was fascinated and made her way quietly closer, being careful to keep out of sight.

It wasn't until she was quite close that she realised just how strange the people looked. They were all tall and slender. The men were all handsome, and the women were graceful and beautiful. Several strange lights flittered into the clearing. They glowed brightly and seemed to grow. Once the light dimmed, Ella realised that people had appeared where the lights had been. The new ladies all had long hair that flowed down past their waists and dresses made of fine fabric that looked like petals. Suddenly, Ella knew what she was looking at.

"Fairies," she whispered to herself, staring in awe.

The fairies kept coming, and soon the glade was full of laughter. The band struck up a tune, and beautiful music began to fill the air. Ella sat watching from the shadows of the woodland. The dancing began, and it was magical to watch. Ella stared in amazement, wishing she could move the way those dancers did. She was so fascinated by them that she didn't even notice the bright light appear behind her until a soft, gentle voice addressed her.

"Hello."

Ella spun around in shock. A tall, elegant woman was standing before her. Her long golden hair fell in waves down past her waist, and she was wearing a long, shimmering cream dress and a small crown of gold on her head. Ella was frightened at first and looked down at her shoes, but when she glanced up, she saw the lady smile at her. She suddenly felt unafraid.

"I'm sorry I intruded," Ella said in a quiet voice.

The lady laughed. The sound reminded Ella of chiming bells. "It's alright, child, but why are you alone in the woods?"

"I love the woods," Ella explained. "When I have a problem, I come to the woods to think." She absently wondered why she was opening up and telling this strange lady everything. She didn't feel shy around her, like she usually was. The lady nodded as if she understood.

"I understand. I do that, too." She smiled and sat down on a stone near Ella. "What is your name?"

"Ella," Ella replied quietly.

"That is a very pretty name. My name is Titania. What troubles brought you to the woods on the day of our festival, Ella?"

Ella looked down at her feet. She took a deep breath and told Titania all about the party and how nervous she was about going. She told her how she didn't know anyone who would be there and how she was afraid she'd embarrass herself since she didn't know how to dance. Titania sat quietly and listened as Ella talked, then stood up from the rock she was sitting on. She held her hand out to Ella.

"Would you like to go to our party? We don't normally invite mortals, but I like you. I will teach you to dance."

Ella looked up and smiled. She took Titania's hand and followed her into the glade. Surprisingly, all the other fairies bowed as they entered. Ella looked up, confused, but Titania laughed and smiled.

"Fairies, let our party begin!" Titania called out.

The music began again, and the fairies started to dance. Titania introduced Ella to many of them and, as she had promised, she taught her how to dance. Ella had an amazing time and wasn't scared at all. She talked to many of the fairies, danced, drank, and ate some of the most amazing food she had ever had. Eventually, though, it was time to go home. Titania walked Ella to the edge of the glade.

"Thank you so much," Ella said. "I had a wonderful time."

"As I am sure you will at your friends' party," Titania replied.

"Oh, I forgot about that," Ella said, looking sad again.

"Remember that you were scared of going because you didn't know anyone? You didn't know anyone here either, yet you were brave and had fun."

"That's true," said Ella with a slight smile.

"And you were afraid you would embarrass yourself because you couldn't dance. Yet, you have danced with us."

"I did, didn't I?" Ella said with a broad smile. "Thank you, Titania."

"You are most welcome," Titania replied.

"My Queen, it is time to go," a fairy called from the stones.

"Queen?" Ella asked. Titania just smiled and stepped back into the glade. A low mist began to rise, and Ella shivered. She turned and walked back towards home. When she glanced back, the glade was empty.

Ella did go to her classmate's party the following weekend. She was brave and tried hard to talk to the other children there. They were all very nice. When the dancing started, she remembered what she had learnt from the fairy queen. Her dancing was so graceful that several of the other girls asked her to teach them, too. Ella was very glad she'd had the courage to go after all.

THE SHARING HAT

Holly the elf was very excited as she walked to school. Autumn leaves fell all around her, and she absently kicked at them as she skipped along. Today was going to be fantastic. It was show-and-tell, and she had the best thing to talk about. The sharing hat. The hat had been a gift from her godmother, Agnes, the witch of the north woods, and it could grant any wish, so long as the wish was shared. Holly thought about all the wonderful wishes she and her classmates could share. Sweets, maybe, or a class trip.

On the way to school, she met some of her friends. As they walked together, each started talking about what they had brought for show-and-tell. Jack proudly showed them a beautiful gemstone that sparkled in the autumn sunshine. Darcy had her dancing shoes, the ones she had worn when she won a prize. May had a fossil she had found with her grandfather. Someone laughed behind them.

"I have something much better than all of those," came the snooty voice of Suzie, another elf in their class.

"What have you brought then?" asked Jack with a sigh. Suzie always had to be better than everyone else, and Jack was fed up with her.

"Not telling," Suzie said, holding her head up higher.

"But it's not as good as what Holly has," Jack bragged. "She has a hat that can grant wishes."

Holly elbowed him. She didn't want Suzie to go telling everyone in class about the hat before she did. It was supposed to be a surprise. Suzie just glared at them all and then walked off, annoyed.

The rest of the morning was full of everyone excitedly waiting for their turn to show what they had brought. Suzie insisted on going first. She had brought her pet squirrel with her. While he was entertaining and cute, he was also very naughty and disruptive. He stole the teacher's chalk and had the whole class chasing him to get it back. Mrs. Oakley called Suzie's parents to come and take him home in the end.

Finally, it was Holly's turn. She took the box with the sharing hat in from her locker. When she opened it, though, the box was empty. Holly searched through her locker, but the hat wasn't there. She started to cry.

"What's the matter, Holly?" Mrs. Oakley asked.

"My magic hat, it's gone!"

The whole class looked for the hat, but it was nowhere to be found. Mrs. Oakley wondered if maybe it had fallen out of the box on the way to school, or at home, but Jack was sure Suzie had taken it.

"I think we should tell Mrs. Oakley," he said.

"But we have no proof!" Darcy pointed out. "It's wrong to accuse people with no proof."

At the end of the day, Holly sadly went home. When she opened the door, she started crying all over again. She knew the hat hadn't fallen out and that someone had probably stolen it. Her mother rushed over, asking her what was the matter. Through her sobs, Holly managed to tell her.

"Not to worry, dearie," said a voice from the doorway. Holly looked up and saw her godmother standing there, smiling.

"But I've lost it."

"Ah, but you didn't tell anyone it was a sharing hat, did you?"

"No," Holly said, confused.

Agnes smiled. "I made the sharing hat with some of my strongest spells. It will misbehave if the thief tries to use it selfishly. It only works if the magic is shared."

"What do you mean 'misbehave'?" asked Holly.

Agnes cackled loudly and smiled as she pulled on her pointed hat and took hold of her broom, ready to leave.

"You'll see," she replied. "I'll be back tomorrow to hear all about it." She stepped out into the autumn evening and climbed onto her broomstick. "Tootles!" she cried as the broom sped away.

Later that night, while Holly lay awake wondering what Agnes meant, Suzie was finding out. She had taken the hat because she wanted to get everything she wished for. When Mrs. Oakley had called her parents to collect her squirrel, she had taken the hat and hidden it with him. As soon as she was home from school, she had fetched the hat and sat on her bed with it.

"I wish I had lots of lovely new dresses," she wished.

"To share with your friends?" the hat asked.

"No," Suzie scoffed.

"Ah," the hat replied. "Very well."

A splendid new dress appeared next to Suzie, but it was too small for her to wear. *Poof* came another, this one too large. Then came more and more and more. Some too short, some too long, some in colours Suzie hated. They piled up and up and up all around her.

"Stop, stop, stop!" she demanded. "You stupid hat. This is all wrong! These dresses are no good, make them go away."

"As you wish," said the hat, and *poof,* they vanished. Or so Suzie thought. In fact, the hat simply moved them into the bathroom.

"I wish I had more toys!" Suzie demanded.

"To share with your family?" asked the hat.

"No!" cried Suzie.

"I see," said the hat.

Toy after toy appeared, but none of them were the sort of thing that Suzie liked. Or if they were, they were too big or too small for her to use.

"Stop, stop, stop!" Suzie yelled. "None of these are any good. Take them away, stupid hat."

Poof, they were gone, this time into the kitchen and her parents' room. Suzie sat crossly on the bed. The hat was useless. She sighed. Then, without thinking, she said, "I'm hungry. I wish I had something to eat."

"I assume not to share," said the hat. "As you wish."

Out of the hat came all sorts of food, but nothing that Suzie liked. Plates of broccoli, bowls of oatmeal, and wobbly pink custard.

"Stop, stop, stop," Suzie cried, but the hat didn't stop.

Instead, the bowls of oatmeal and custard began to overflow and form rivers flowing through her room towards the stairs. Suzie screamed and yelled for the hat to stop as the flow of gloopy pink dotted with floating broccoli bits began to flow into the lounge where her parents were. At the same time, the bathroom door burst open and party dresses of every colour flowed out onto the landing, and piles of toys cascaded from the kitchen. Suzie's parents started shouting and asking what was happening. Suzie told them about the hat and the wishes, too scared to lie about what she had done.

"Well, how do we stop it?" asked her mother.

"Ask the hat," her father said.

They waded upstairs through the gloopy mess to Suzie's room, dragging Suzie with them. Her father pushed his way into the bedroom that was now almost completely filled with pink goo.

"Hat, please stop," he said.

"Won't," said the hat.

"Why not?" asked her mother.

"That snotty girl stole what wasn't hers and doesn't want to share. That's not what mistress made me for."

"Mistress?" asked Suzie's father.

"Mistress Agnes of the north woods," came a laugh from the window.

Suzie's father looked out and saw Holly's godmother floating on her broom outside the window. A broad smile covered her face.

"Oh please, please, tell us how to stop this," Suzie's mother begged.

"Oh, that's easy," said Agnes. "Suzie must take the hat to Holly and say sorry. That will stop the hat from making anything more. Then Suzie must take all the things the hat made and share them. Finally, she must clean up the mess she made."

"But!" Suzie protested, but one look from her mother made her be quiet. Suzie picked up the hat and headed towards Holly's house. Holly was overjoyed to have the hat back, and many of the village children were also delighted with the new party clothes and wonderful toys they received. In fact, everyone was happy except Suzie, but she had learnt two valuable lessons. Firstly, that it is wrong to take what is not yours. Secondly, if you have good fortune, it pays to share it.

THE LAND UNDER THE BED

Lucy's little brother sat on his bed looking miserable. Big, fat tears rolled down his plump little cheeks. It made Lucy feel awful. He was so scared of going to bed, and no matter what their parents tried, it didn't work.

"Please, Lucy," he sobbed. "Stay. Pretty please! They won't get me if you're here."

"Who?" Lucy asked.

Ben looked up at her with big blue eyes and dropped his voice to a whisper. "The monsters under the bed."

Lucy nearly laughed, but one look at Ben's face made her realise he was serious. She smiled at him kindly. So that was what he was afraid of. *Maybe*, she thought, *if I stay with him tonight, I can prove to him that monsters aren't real. Then Ben would be happy, and so would Mum and Dad.*

"Alright," Lucy, standing up. "We'll have a sleepover. I'll go get my sleeping bag and maybe I can have a word with those monsters and tell them to leave you alone."

"You can do that!" Ben said innocently, his mouth hanging open.

"Yes," said Lucy with a nod of her head.

Lucy ran downstairs and explained everything to her parents, then went to her own room to fetch her pillow and sleeping bag. She didn't believe in monsters, but just in case she also brought along Fidget, her fluffy toy rabbit, and her torch.

Once Mum and Dad had read them a story and everyone was tucked in for the night, Mum turned on the nightlight. She and Dad said goodnight and closed the door, leaving Lucy and Ben alone. Lucy had never slept in Ben's room before. It was lovely during the day, with big pictures of farm animals all around the walls. In the dim blue glow of the night light, though, it wasn't quite as nice. Lucy thought about her own room with its powder pink walls and soft bed. She absently pulled Fidget closer. Then she nearly laughed. She was spooking herself.

"Alright then, Ben. Tell me about these monsters," she said.

Ben pushed himself up in his cot bed and looked down at her. He seemed a lot happier since she had agreed to stay with him.

"They don't come out until after they think I'm asleep," Ben whispered. "But I hear them."

Lucy smiled. "Alright, you get to sleep, I'll stay awake."

Ben sighed, turned over, and curled up under his blanket. Lucy lay back on her camp mattress. It was surprisingly comfortable. She stared up at the ceiling. Like hers, it was covered in glow-in-the-dark stars. It was pretty. Lucy wasn't sure how long she'd been looking at them, but just as she was starting to fall asleep, she heard a noise. A small shuffling noise coming from under the bed. Suddenly, she tensed. Could Ben be right? Could there really be monsters under the bed? No, monsters weren't real. There had to be a logical explanation.

Lucy took a firm grip of her torch, flicked it on, and shone it straight at Ben's bed. She wasn't sure what to expect. Her imagination thought it was possibly a scary monster, but her rational mind said it was more likely a mouse. She was not expecting what she saw. There, in front of her, was a small furry brown and white creature about the size of a teacup. It had huge brown eyes, little furry hands, and a rather flat, round face.

"EEK!" it screamed. "Human!"

Lucy snapped out of the trance she'd found herself in at the creature's screech. It seemed that whatever it was, it was as scared of them as Ben was of it. The furball's shout had woken Ben, who immediately looked at it and flung himself into the corner of his cot bed, pulling the blanket over his head.

"Get it, Lucy, get it!" he hollered.

Lucy just started to laugh. Ben was hiding under his blanket and the creature was almost mirroring him, hiding under one of Ben's socks. The sound of Lucy laughing made Ben peek out from under his blanket and the little monster look out from under its sock.

"It's not funny!" the little monster huffed. "You'd be scared if someone shone a light on you in the dark when you weren't expecting it."

"Sorry," Lucy said, lowering the torch. "But it's not nice to make strange noises in the dark and scare children either."

The little monster followed her gaze as she looked at Ben, who was still huddled up with the blankets pulled high under his chin.

"But he's always asleep when we come out, isn't he?"

"No," Ben said.

"We?" Lucy asked.

The little monster took a deep breath and sat down beside the sock she had been carrying. Lucy lowered the torch a little more and gently pulled Ben down from his bed. That way, he could see the little creature was not scary.

"We live under the floorboards. We're house monsters."

"Do you eat children?" Ben asked.

The little creature looked shocked. "No! Do you suck house monsters up in vacuum cleaners to sell to toymakers?"

"No," said Lucy.

The little creature tilted her head. "Are you sure?"

"Well, we have a vacuum cleaner, but it's for sucking up dirt, not monsters. We didn't even know you existed. Ben just heard you in the night and thought you were going to hurt him."

"Oh no," said the monster with a little laugh. "We come out at night to find food and sometimes to borrow socks." She waved the sock in her hand.

"What's your name? I'm Lucy, and this is Ben."

"My name is Cotton."

"Do you really live under the bed?" Ben asked, suddenly feeling brave.

"Yep. Do you want to see?"

"Yes, please! But how would we fit?" asked Lucy.

"Oh, I can shrink you, just for a little bit. You'd go back to full size in an hour. We use the shrinking potion to make things small when we need to fit them through holes."

Without another word, Cotton threw a sparkling powder over Lucy and Ben. Lucy felt a strange tickling all over her and realised that everything around her seemed to be getting bigger and bigger. Or rather, she was getting smaller and smaller. Soon enough, she and Ben were the same size as Cotton.

"This way," Cotton said, leading the way under the bed.

Lucy held tightly to Ben's hand. She was very proud of how brave he was being. There were lots of things under Ben's bed. Soon enough, he was more interested in the lost toys he found than in the fact he had been made tiny. As they walked along, Cotton pointed out lots of things about the "underbed." She took them past the "statue," which Lucy recognised as one of Ben's toy soldiers, and led them to the "duck door." This was a small hole in the floor close to the duck painting on the wall. They paused by the hole, and Lucy watched in mild disgust as Cotton picked up a ball of dust from the floor and popped it into her mouth.

"Yum," she said. "Oh, sorry, that was rude. Did you want some?"

"No, thanks," Lucy said.

"You eat dust?" Ben said. "Yuk!"

Cotton just shrugged and waved them through the hole. They emerged into the darkness of the underfloor. Lucy had expected it to be grubby, but it was spotlessly clean and shiny. There were lots of little monsters going about their work. Some were wearing hard hats made of old egg cups, some were dragging socks full of lint, which Cotton said was their main food.

"Sometimes, we get the crumbs of a cookie. They are a special treat," she added.

Cotton showed them her home. It was an area marked off with cardboard walls. She had a bed made of a matchbox and a sock, a table made of an old cotton reel (which had also given her mother the inspiration for her name), and even an old dollhouse chair to sit on.

Ben and Lucy loved seeing the world under the floor and spending time with Cotton. She introduced them to lots of other little monsters. When they met the baby monsters, Ben thought they were so cute he swore he would never be afraid of the monsters under the bed again.

Eventually, though, Cotton said their shrinking potion would wear off soon and took them back up into Ben's room. Ben was really tired and climbed into bed straight away. He pulled his cover over him and rubbed his eyes sleepily.

"Goodnight, Lucy. Goodnight, Cotton," he mumbled as his eyes closed.

"Goodnight, Ben," Lucy replied. "Thank you, Cotton."

"Eh, no problem. It's nice to know that humans don't really sell us to toy companies."

Cotton headed back under the bed as Lucy climbed into her sleeping bag, feeling tired herself. The next morning, the sunlight streaming through the window woke Lucy up. She stretched and laughed at the strange dream about travelling under the bed with Ben's monsters. Ben stirred in his own bed.

"Morning, Lucy."

"Morning, Ben."

"Wasn't last night amazing?" Ben said. "Meeting Cotton and shrinking." Lucy gasped. Had she and Ben had the same dream? It couldn't be real, could it?

"I'm going to get a cookie and put it under the bed tonight," Ben said as he climbed out of bed. "For Cotton, to say thank you. And thank you, Lucy, for being the bravest, best big sister ever."

Ben climbed onto Lucy's knee and gave her a big hug. It didn't matter if it was real or not. Ben was no longer afraid of the monsters under the bed, and that was what mattered. *Just in case, though*, Lucy thought, *I might just put a cookie under my bed too!*

MERRI AND THE MAKE-BELIEVE DRAGON

Merri was sitting beside the village fountain, reading a book. Several other children were playing with a ball in the sunshine. It was a lovely day. Merri was just about to put her book down and join them when a few younger children came running over to her.

"Merri, Merri, tell us a story, pleeeaasse!" they begged.

Merri smiled. She loved telling stories and reading to the younger children in the village. Tales of princesses and knights were usually the most popular. She put her book aside and began telling the children one of her favourite stories, all about a magic sword. The children listened to her intently, and by the time she got to the part about the dragon, the group was even bigger. Merri enjoyed embellishing her stories, making them sound even more exciting, and she was very good at it.

By the time she reached the end of the story, the children playing with the ball had stopped their game to listen. Even a couple of passing adults were looking on with mild interest. When she finished, she stood up to go home.

"Oh, are you going? Can't you tell us another story?" a little boy asked.

"Yeah, we want to know more about the dragon!" another said.

Merri wasn't exactly sure why she said what she did next, but it made life very interesting for a while.

"Oh, if you want to know about dragons, you should go to the cave by the woods. That's where they live."

The children murmured among themselves. "Really?" one asked.

Merri giggled. "Yes, they live in the cave. I've seen them. Haven't you heard the strange noises that come from there?"

Some of the children looked a little worried, some laughed and said Merri was making it up, but the two little boys she had been speaking to looked so excited they could pop. Merri smiled. She liked seeing the younger children excited by her stories. She started to gather her books up to go home, and most of the children began to wander away, but the two little boys stayed, whispering together. Merri could just make out what they were saying.

"Let's go see if it's a real dragon," one said.

"Yeah! I want to see a dragon," the other replied.

Merri smiled to herself. She thought she had a great idea. She threw her books into her bag and headed out away from the village. It was a lovely warm day, and Merri ran her hands through the long green grass as she walked along the footpath towards the woods. She was well ahead of the two boys, and she knew a shortcut through the woods to the cave. Once inside the shade of the trees, she made her way quickly off the path. Hopping over a fallen log, she picked her way carefully to the cave.

She slipped inside the cool, dark cave and hid behind a rock at the entrance. She could barely contain her laughter as she hid in the darkness. This would be such a good laugh and it would make her stories so much better. She waited quietly. Soon enough, she heard the sound of the two boys coming up the hill towards the cave. When she guessed they were close enough, she cupped her hands around her mouth and faced into the cave so it would sound louder, then let out the loudest roar she could.

"Did you hear that?" she heard one boy hiss.

"No," said the other, but his voice wobbled as he said it.

Merri giggled just a little and let out another roar. This time, she heard someone yell "Dragon" and "Run." She peeped out from behind the rock just in time to see the boys running away from the cave. Merri laughed so hard her sides hurt, and she kept giggling all the way home.

Merri didn't think much more about her joke until the next day when she headed into the village to collect a new book. A large crowd of children had gathered around the two boys at the fountain. One of them saw her and pointed, jumping up and down.

"Merri, Merri, we heard the dragon!"

"Oh," said Merri with a smile.

"They don't believe us, but it's true. Tell them, Merri."

Merri was about to tell them it was all a story and that she was sorry for scaring them when two older boys about Merri's age wandered over.

"Dragons aren't real," one said.

"And even if they were, we wouldn't be scared," the other said with a laugh. "We're not girls!"

Merri felt a little annoyed at the boys. "Really? Big fire-breathing, knight-eating dragons don't scare you, do they? Maybe you should prove it!"

The older boys didn't like being challenged. "I'll go now," said one. The other nodded his agreement. Soon enough, a whole crowd of children were heading towards the woods. Once again, Merri slipped off the main track and hurried along her shortcut to the cave. She wasn't sure that a simple roar would scare the older boys, but she was determined to do something.

Once in the cave, she gathered some dry sticks and lit a fire behind her hiding rock. Just as the sound of the crowd floated into the cave, she threw on some damp leaves and smoke streamed from the fire upward and out of the cave. Merri immediately made her roar, louder and fiercer than the day before.

"Look, smoke!" someone yelled.

"Listen to that roar!" said another.

"We told you it was a dragon!"

"Aren't you going in?" a voice asked.

Merri peeped out from behind the rock. The two older boys stood looking pale in front of the cave. Merri tried not to laugh and let out another big roar. The two boys turned on their heels and ran, and the rest of the children quickly followed them. Merri laughed until she cried. "I'm not a girl!" she said to herself imitating one of the boys, and she laughed again.

Merri skipped back home and went in for tea. She found her mother and father looking very worried. Her mother hugged her tight as soon as she came through the door. "Oh, Merri. I'm so glad you are safe," she said.

"Safe?" Merri asked.

"Now, Merri," her father said, "we need you to watch your baby brother tonight. There is a village meeting. Lock the door when we go and don't open it or go outside for anything. Do you understand?"

Merri nodded. She was suddenly scared. What could be so bad that there was going to be a village meeting? What was so dangerous she couldn't go outside?

"Wh-what is the meeting for?" she asked.

"We don't want to scare you," her mother said.

"She should know," her father said. "Some of the children claim there is a beast in the cave behind the village."

Merri stared at her father, suddenly even more worried. She hadn't meant her joke to go this far. It was one thing to play a practical joke on the other children, but this was getting out of hand. Merri wondered what to do. She didn't want her parents to get mad at her, but she didn't want the whole village to be afraid of something that wasn't real either. She wondered briefly if she could do nothing. Maybe the grown-ups would go and see the cave and realise nothing was there and it would be OK. No, that would be cowardly, and she wasn't a coward.

"Mother, Father," Merri said quietly. "I think I should tell you something."

She sat down at the table and told her parents everything. All about the story and the dragon and the joke. About the two mean boys and how she had scared them. Her parents were mad, but they were also very proud of how brave Merri was at confessing and telling the truth. Her father took her to the town meeting so she could explain to the other grown-ups that there was no beast and they didn't need to worry. Merri felt embarrassed doing it, but nowhere near as embarrassed as the two older boys who thought they were so brave but had fallen for her story. And Merri? Well, she still tells stories by the fountain, but she is always clear to remind her audience that they aren't real. She always tells the truth, and she doesn't play pranks anymore.

RACHEL TO THE RESCUE

Rachel hugged Uncle Mike goodbye and climbed onto the school bus. School trips were always exciting, but she'd still have rather spent the day with Uncle Mike. He was so cool. She slipped into her seat and waved at him out of the window. Uncle Mike knew everything about the woods and living in them. He'd been in the army when he was younger, and he was determined to teach her how to take care of herself. Rachel smiled, thinking back to their latest trip to the woods. He'd shown her how to make a camp and start a fire, and he'd even given her a present. She pulled his old compass out of her jacket pocket and rubbed her finger over the brass case before testing the brand-new torch he'd given her too.

"Alright, children. Take your seats," Mrs. Willis shouted.

Everyone sat down, still chatting loudly. Jake sat down beside Rachel. They usually sat together because he was as quiet as she was. He smiled at her a little.

"Did you have fun with your uncle?" he asked.

"Yeah." Rachel nodded and showed him the compass.

The historical site they were visiting was quite far from school, and the bus trundled along a forest trail most of the way. Rachel stared out at it, wishing she was walking among the quiet trees rather than sitting on the noisy bus. The field trip itself was uneventful. As usual, several of the boys caused trouble, several of the girls were totally disinterested, and Rachel wandered around with Jake, keeping out of the way.

Eventually, they were all ushered back onto the bus for the journey home. It was late autumn, so the sun was beginning to go down by the time they entered the forest road. Many of the children were being loud. Someone started throwing balls of paper, and Mrs. Willis shouted at them. Then, out of nowhere, there was a loud bang. The bus began to wobble and shake. It swerved across the road and off into the trees. It bounced and jolted until it eventually came to rest, the front end crushed against a tall pine tree. Mrs. Willis stood up quickly.

"Is everyone OK? Mr. Brown?"

"I'm OK. We blew a tyre," the driver called back.

"Alright, everyone off the bus. Let's check everyone over," Mrs. Willis ordered.

Everyone marched off the bus. There were a few scratches, but most people were just shaken up. The same could not be said for the bus. Its front end was crumpled up against the tree.

"Well, we'd better get walking," Mrs. Willis said with a sigh. "It's getting dark, and that bus isn't going to start."

"Is that what we should do?" Jake hissed in Rachel's ear. She shook her head a little. It was definitely not what her uncle would have done. "Tell her!"

"I can't. She's our teacher," Rachel said nervously.

"Go on." Jake pushed her.

"OK." Rachel took a deep breath. "Miss."

"Yes, Rachel?"

"Erm, it's just, um…"

"What Rachel?" Mrs. Willis asked, a little anxiously.

Rachel took a deep breath. She knew exactly what to do. This was what her uncle had been teaching her about. It didn't matter how nervous she was, she had to do this.

"We need to stay with the vehicle. In case of an accident, always stay with the vehicle. It's bigger than you, and someone will be searching your route for it. The way to stay safe is to stay with it. If your vehicle isn't visible, then leave a marker," she said, reciting what her uncle had said. "Everyone knows where we were going. When we don't get back on time, they'll come this way. If we stay with the bus, we'll be found. We should take some of the hi-vis vests and hang them on the road where we came off, so anyone driving past will see them."

Mrs. Willis stopped and looked at her, one eyebrow raised. "Alright," she said with a smile. "Jake, Isla, Claire, take a few of the hi-vis vests and hang them on the trees where we came off the road. Anything else?"

Everyone was looking at Rachel. She swallowed. "If we have a medical kit, we should make sure any cuts and scrapes are clean. We should check there's no leak in the petrol tank too. If it's safe, we can all stay on the bus, maybe wrap up warm."

"I'll check the bus," said Mr. Brown. "I have a torch."

Mrs. Willis and Rachel checked over any cuts and scrapes. Mr. Brown and the other children came back. It was getting dark and the wind was starting to pick up, making it chilly.

"I'm not sure about a leak." Mr. Brown said. "I think it's OK, but…"

"Mr. Brown, do you have a tarp or anything on the bus?" Rachel asked.

"I do. Why?"

"Can I borrow it, please?" Rachel asked.

Mr. Brown fetched the big trap from a hatch under the bus. Rachel grabbed Jake and had him help her spread it out. Remembering what her uncle had taught her, she used some branches and bandages from the medical kit to string it up as a windbreak. Everyone huddled behind it, out of the wind. Mr. Brown sat at one end with his torch, and Rachel sat at the other, her own torch set to flash to save the batteries.

"We should play a game," Rachel said. "Keep our minds busy."

"It's not going to be I-spy, it's too dark," Claire moaned.

"I know!" Jake said. "My name is Andy. I come from Andalusia and I like apples."

A few laughs erupted from the others, but one by one they started playing the game. Rachel wasn't sure how long they'd been playing when she heard her name being called. At first, she thought it was her imagination, but then she heard it again. This time, she knew who was calling her.

"Uncle Mike!" she shouted, leaping up to her feet and snapping on the torch fully. "Over here, we're over here."

A few moments later, Uncle Mike appeared with several policemen and parents. He wrapped Rachel in a blanket and gave her a big hug.

"Is anyone hurt?" a policeman asked.

"No, thanks to Rachel." Jake piped up.

Uncle Mike looked down at her and then at the tarp and smiled. "That's my girl."

Everyone got home safely later that night. They all got the next day off too. When they went back to school, there was a special assembly and Rachel got a special award.

The headmaster even asked Uncle Mike to come to school and talk to everyone about safety and survival. It was a very good thing that Rachel overcame her shyness to help save the day. She was very brave.

THE MYSTERY COMIC BOOK

Cara tucked her long blonde hair behind her ear as she pulled open her locker. The school corridor was busy. and almost everyone in it said good morning to her. Someone had just invited her to a party, and her friend Casey had just asked her to be part of the dance committee. It looked like it was going to be a busy week. She turned around to head towards her first class when she saw a girl from the year below her trip and fall, scattering her books across the floor. Several of the boys laughed. Cara sighed, then stepped forward and helped the girl up before gathering her books up.

"Thank you!" the girl said, surprised. Cara smiled. She may have been the most popular girl in school, but that didn't mean she was unkind. The boys stopped laughing openly, but she could see them giggling among themselves. She rolled her eyes.

"Hey, Cara. You want to go to the dance with me?" one asked.

"No," she replied sharply. There was no way she'd ever go out with someone who laughed at someone else's misfortune. She turned around and walked away towards class, hearing the other boys teasing their rejected friend.

"Harsh rejection," a voice said behind her.

Cara turned around and saw her friend Reed making his way towards her, navigating his wheelchair through the group of people still milling around the corridor.

"Was I too mean?" she asked, suddenly feeling guilty.

"Nah, I have PE with that guy. He's mean." Reed smiled. Cara smiled back.

"So, who are you planning on going to the dance with?" she asked Reed.

"Wait, we're going? We're not shunning it and eating pizza?"

"Not this time," Cara said. "I'm on the committee."

Reed sighed. "Dancing isn't my strong suit," he said, spinning around on his wheels.

"Looked like a dance move to me," she replied.

The news that Cara was officially going to the dance spread around the school by the end of the day, and she'd been asked out five times. None of the guys who asked her knew anything about her, though, and most didn't seem to want to find out what she thought about things either. She'd complained to Reed and Casey about it at lunch, jokingly pointing out it was Casey's fault.

"I'll go get you pudding," Reed had said, heading off towards the food counter.

"You want me to spread it around school that we were obsessed with comic books when we were little?" Casey asked.

Cara laughed. "You want to say that a little louder? I don't think they heard you in the staffroom."

The rest of the day was more of the same, and by the time she headed home that night she was miserable. She lay in her room, wondering if she'd ever meet a nice guy. Someone who liked her for being her, not because she was pretty and popular. Then she turned over and pulled her blankets up close. Feeling sorry for herself was silly. Other kids at school had real problems. At least no one ever teased her.

The next morning, Cara was at school early. She made her way to her locker, determined to be cheerful. Casey was waiting in the library for her to go over plans for the dance, but it was the last thing Cara really wanted to think about. She opened her locker and was just about to stuff her books inside when she noticed a sheet of paper wedged inside the door. Pulling it out, Cara unfolded the paper. Surprisingly, it had a comic strip on it. Cara giggled. Casey had gone all out on this joke. There was a cartoon superhero of someone who looked just like her helping a girl pick up her books and using some kind of heat ray on a boy picking on her.

Cara wandered into the library, smiling broadly. Casey was sitting at one of the large wooden tables, surrounded by paper, a pencil wedged in her curly red hair. Without a word, Cara sat down beside her and dropped the comic strip in front of her friend.

"What's this?" Casey asked, picking it up.

"Like you don't know. Give it up, Case. I'll give you this, you're way better at art than I thought."

"I didn't do this!" Casey said.

"Right," Cara said sarcastically.

"Best friends honour. I didn't do this, Car, I swear," Casey said, putting her hand over her heart.

Cara glanced back at the cartoon. Casey wouldn't lie to her, even for a joke. So, if Casey hasn't done it, who had? Someone from the canteen who had heard them talking?

Cara spent most of the day wondering who had sent her the comic. Casey had asked everyone she could think of, which had made Cara smile. Casey didn't seem to have a filter button when it came to finding things out. At the end of the day, she went to gather her belongings from her locker and found a note inside.

"I guess you liked my comic. Not all guys are the same, you know. Some of us don't suck." It was signed with a simple smiley face. Cara read it, then read it again. Some guy had sent her a comic book to cheer her up.

Over the next week, Cara got more and more pages of her comic book self. Whoever was making them seemed to know her really well. They knew her favourite colour was purple, that she liked chocolate and ice cream, hated bullying, and even that her favourite subject was English. Anyone who paid any attention would know those things, but who was it?

The dance was getting closer, but all Cara could think about was finding out who was sending her the comics. When she was sad, they made her feel better. She really wanted to talk to whoever was making them. Maybe whoever it was would ask her to the dance she thought one night as she sat staring at a page. Then she stopped herself. What was she thinking? She had no idea who it was, and yet she wanted to go to the dance with them. She sighed.

Finally, with no idea about what else to do, she pinned a note to her locker. It said *Hey comic book guy, do you want to dance?* When she went to her locker at the end of the day, she was sad to see no reply and no new page. Cara felt suddenly sad. Maybe it had been a cruel joke. She closed her locker, feeling embarrassed, and ran home.

When she went to the locker the next morning, there was still no note and no page. Cara closed her locker sadly. It had been a joke, and she'd fallen for it.

"Hey." Cara turned around to see Reed. She tried to smile.

"Hey," she replied.

"What's wrong?"

"Nothing," Cara replied. "It's just… I thought the guy, the comic guy… I thought maybe he liked me and, well, I guess it was all just a joke."

Reed suddenly looked guilty. "Cara, maybe whoever it was just didn't think you'd really want to go to the dance with them if you knew who it was."

"Thanks for trying to cheer me up," Cara said with a smile.

"Seriously, Car? You really want to go to the dance with this guy?"

"I did before I found out it was a joke," she replied.

"What if he couldn't dance?"

Cara laughed. "I don't care if he's an embarrassing dancer. You know me better than that."

"Yeah, I do. What if he can't dance at all?"

Reed glanced down at his legs. Someone who knew her and knew her well. Someone who knew what she liked, someone who couldn't dance.

"You?" Cara asked, realisation hitting her. Reed nodded. Cara smiled broadly. She crouched down next to Reed.

"I don't care if he can't dance at all." She reached her arms around Reed and hugged him tightly.

"Then I guess I'm gonna need a suit since I'm taking the prettiest girl in school to the dance." Reed smiled, pulled her onto his knee, and wheeled her along the corridor to class as she laughed and giggled.

FOR THE LOVE OF A PONY

Anna loved riding at her local stables. She loved all the horses, but her favourite pony was a stocky little black cob called Storm. He wasn't the prettiest pony at the riding school, but he was so sweet and gentle. He had become Anna's best friend. Storm didn't belong to Jane, who owned the riding school; she had him on loan from a local farmer whose daughter had outgrown him.

One Saturday morning, while she was helping to clean the stables, Anna overheard Jane talking to one of the older girls about Storm.

"Well, he'll be a loss for sure, but Farmer Dray wants to sell him and I don't have the money to buy him right now, not with the barn roof needing to be repaired," Jane said.

"Can't we ask him to wait a few months so we can save up the money?" the older girl asked, looking a little sad.

Jane shook her head. "I asked that, but Mr. Dray is selling up and retiring."

"Some of the girls will be upset," the older girl said.

She was right, and one of them was Anna. She waited until Jane and the girl left, then snuck out of the stall and found Storm in his stable. Wrapping her arms around his neck, she buried her face in his mane.

"Don't worry, Storm. I'll keep you here, somehow."

Anna was very quiet at supper time and didn't really want her food. She just shuffled it around her plate with her fork. Her father noticed how strangely she was behaving and asked her about it, but when she told him, he dismissed her.

"Oh, Anna, it's just one pony. There are others at the stable."

"Not like Storm," Anna replied.

Anna didn't sleep very well that night, but when she got up in the morning, she had a plan. She rushed to the stables early, well before her lesson, and found Jane. She was in the hay barn, filling up nets for the morning. Anna started to help.

"Jane?"

"Yes," Jane replied without looking up from the net she was filling.

"I-I know about Storm." Jane stopped and looked up at Anna with a sad smile. "I heard you talking. Jane, how much would we need to keep Storm?"

Jane sighed. "Eight hundred pounds."

Anna tried not to cry. That was a lot of money. "How long?"

"He goes up for sale next month," Jane replied honestly.

Anna nodded her head slowly. After her lesson, Anna headed straight home. She found her small money box and checked how much was in it. Her mother came in as she was counting out the last of it.

"Mum, do you have any chores I could do to earn a little extra pocket money?" Anna asked.

Her mum smiled. "Well, I'm sure I do. What's this about?"

"I'm going to earn enough money to buy Storm for the school," Anna said with determination.

"How much will you need?"

"Eight hundred pounds," Anna said, looking down. "But I have fifty I saved from Christmas and my birthday."

Anna's mum smiled. She was very proud of her daughter. "I tell you what, I know Mrs. Everly next door needs her yard swept and her grass cutting, why don't you ask her, too? I'll pay you to put out the washing, bring it in, and fold it."

"Thank you!" Anna jumped up and hugged her mum.

Anna worked very hard over the next four weeks. After she had swept Mrs. Everly's yard, the kind old lady asked what she was saving for. When she heard what Anna was up to, she not only gave her a little extra money for the chores but also told her that her daughter was looking for a babysitter, if she was interested. Anna ended up babysitting for several other mothers, too.

The Friday before Storm was to be put up for sale, Anna sat in the kitchen counting up everything she had earned. Her mum and dad came in just as she was finishing. She looked so sad, her mother asked her what was wrong.

"I worked so hard," she said, starting to cry. "But I only made £450. It's not enough."

"Well, just because Storm is going up for sale, it doesn't mean someone will buy him straight away," Mum said.

That was true. There was still a chance. Anna wiped her eyes and sniffed a little. She would keep trying. She couldn't give up on Storm. She wouldn't.

"Do you have any chores, Dad?" Anna asked.

"The car could do with a good clean," her dad replied. Before he could say anything else, Anna ran off to get a bucket and sponge.

The following weekend, having worked hard again all week, Anna headed to the stables for her lesson. Jane was there as usual.

"I'm up to £490 now. Over halfway!" Anna said happily.

Jane lowered her eyes a little. "Anna, I'm sorry."

"What?" Anna asked, suddenly afraid.

"I had a call from Mr. Dray. Storm's been sold, honey. I don't know who to."

Anna didn't know what to say. She turned and ran all the way home, tears streaming down her face. She rushed through the kitchen, past Mum, and straight to her room. How could Storm have been sold? What would she do without him? Would his new owner be nice to him? She felt like her world was falling apart and there was nothing she could do to stop it.

"Anna?" her mum called from downstairs.

Anna didn't answer. She was too upset to see anyone and the thought of having to explain what had happened just made her heart ache. She cried into her pillow, wishing that somehow it was wrong, that he hadn't been sold. She heard the sound of someone on the stairs, then her bedroom door opened slowly.

"Anna?" Mum said.

"Please go away, Mum. I want to be on my own," she sobbed, her face still pressed into the pillow.

"We thought you'd like to know about Storm," Dad said. She hadn't even realised he was there. Wait, did he know who'd bought Storm?

Slowly, she sat up. Her cheeks were wet from her tears, so she wiped them with her sleeve and tried not to burst out crying again. She swallowed and braced herself for what her father was about to say.

"Y-you know who bought him?" she asked, her voice shaky.

"Yes." Dad nodded and smiled. "It was me."

Anna sat stunned, not quite sure she had heard her father right. "You?"

Dad laughed. "Yes, me. Or rather, Mum and me. We were so impressed by how hard you worked, Anna. You remember I said if I thought you could be responsible for a pony, I would consider getting you one? Well, you proved yourself."

"You mean… Storm is mine!" Anna said in disbelief.

"All yours. I went to the stables to ask Jane if we could keep him there while you continue your lessons. I was going to surprise you, but I guess you got there before me," Dad said.

"Oh, Mum, Dad, thank you!" Anna leapt up from the bed and hugged her parents tightly.

"Mind you keep your school work up. Any slipping of that and I might change my mind," Dad said.

"I promise. I'll do all my homework and do the best I can."

"That's all we ask," said Mum.

"Oh!" Anna picked up her money tin and handed it to her dad. "I guess this is yours."

Dad laughed. "You better keep that. You might need it for carrots."

Anna smiled and hugged her parents again.

"I think it's about time we go and meet the newest member of the family, don't you?" Mum said. Anna nodded in agreement. She was nearly crying again, but this time with joy.

Anna was so happy to see Storm that she ran across the yard and wrapped her arms around him.

"Oh, Storm, I did it. I promised I would. I worked hard, and it paid off. You're going to stay with me forever, I promise."

Storm nuzzled her with his soft black velvet nose and rubbed his ear on her shoulder. It was as if he understood he was home and no one was going to take him from the girl who loved him the most in all the world. Mum and Dad stood with Jane, all smiling. It was the best day ever, and it only got better when Jane brought over Storm's tack and Anna got to ride him for the first time as her very own pony. Anna will never forget that working hard is the best way to get what you want, and Storm will always be there to remind her, just in case.

DISCLAIMER

This book contains opinions and ideas of the author and is meant to teach the reader informative and helpful knowledge while due care should be taken by the user in the application of the information provided. The instructions and strategies are possibly not right for every reader and there is no guarantee that they work for everyone. Using this book and implementing the information/recipes therein contained is explicitly your own responsibility and risk. This work with all its contents, does not guarantee correctness, completion, quality or correctness of the provided information. Misinformation or misprints cannot be completely eliminated.

Printed in Great Britain
by Amazon